PRODIGAL SON

Also by John Wheatcroft

DEATH OF A CLOWN

OFOETI (*Alcoa Playwriting Award; NET Playhouse; National Educational Television Award*)

PRODIGAL SON

By John Wheatcroft

Thomas Yoseloff

New York • South Brunswick • London

© 1967 by John Wheatcroft
Library of Congress Catalogue Card Number: 67-25168

Thomas Yoseloff, Publisher
Cranbury, N. J. 08512

Thomas Yoseloff Ltd
18 Charing Cross Road
London W.C.2, England

6734
Printed in the United States of America

ACKNOWLEDGMENTS

Some of these poems, a number of them under other titles, have appeared in *Approach, Artesian, The Beloit Poetry Journal, The Carleton Miscellany, The Colorado Quarterly, The Dalhousie Review, The Educational Forum, Envoi, Forum* (Ball State University), *Four Quarters, The Georgia Review,* the *New York Herald Tribune, The Minnesota Review, The North Dakota Quarterly, South And West, The University Review.*

"Magnolia Blooms," © 1966, The Curtis Publishing Company.

"George Weimar Who Taught Me Chess," Headless Fisherman on Long Beach Island at Sunset," "Winter Missive," © 1965/66/67 by The New York Times Company.

ACKNOWLEDGMENTS

CONTENTS

7

TO MY MOTHER AND FATHER

ANATHEMA: FOR THE BOMBERS OF LAMBS

Birmingham, Alabama
Sunday, September 15, 1963

Light a liquid fire, Lord, within my mouth.

Their offering (burnt) on this Communion Day
resurrects the cannibal in me . . .
now I could drink cold blood, devour inhuman flesh.

For the sake of Jesus lover of all kids
let no one simpering say
"These did not die in vain."
And let no brother turn his other cheek,
no father dare forgive them
 (for they knew what they did),
no mother yield another lamb for burning.

I pray each little black-charred bone tattoo
perpetually against the membrane that
their shriveled hearts be stretched to,
tenter-hooked across the bottoms
of their hollow skulls;
I pray a tide of boiling children's blood
seethe their naked nerves throughout eternity.

Such sacrifice eats up all love
it takes to shape a human heaven,
rekindles in dampered hearts
old fires of hell.

HITTING A PHEASANT ON THE
PENNSYLVANIA TURNPIKE

Bird want? hen fear? maybe one
of those little earthquakes in the heart
that scoot men too?—for I was driving,
restless between two points of rest.
Curiosity before conscience plunges us
brain-first into history after causes.

Rats master mazes; our human Doom—
re-live. Thus: angling from the camouflage
of cornstubs she arrows in the slit
where see begins, sheer motion;
quicker than think she aggravates
to looming wings; zaps matter
against the windshield, shatterproof—
even our eyes we've armored past armadillos'—
before my foot can jump from zoom
to stop; then bursts so big she's gone.

Fear flares cold nerves like circuited toaster wires.
Yet catching her crazy flutter on the concrete
in my rearview mirror, not dying raw
but dying's dumb show on a two-dimensional screen,
I've been conditioned man enough to boot
the sagging needle back to seventy-five.

Perhaps she's weighty with unborn birds,
sacrificing lift for life. Why not program
Pavlovian safety lessons for fledging pheasants?
breed in "need-speed gear," "superheft"?

13

The film runs out, half my schizophrenic eye
witnessing her technicolor finish
by a trailing Buick—green
in a brown-feathered squall.
A nimble natural lawyer would evince
contributory negligence;
a Coke and Blackstone stickler force
dismissal on the technicality.

So, judge in me acquits me, with some wisdom:
Guilt is one recreation we can't afford.
Our manufacture does the killing. Collisions
are time's complicities, history's physics.
Only an aggrandizing superego will
projectile causes from the unfortuitous concourse
of trajectories that claimed one female pheasant life
along the Pennsylvania Turnpike back
to Hiroshima, Bay of Pigs, and momently to Hanoi.

KAMIKAZE

*Japanese Flag Painted on the Bridge
of the U.S.S. Yorktown, August 5, 1945*

Wait three days. Report
then to my father, gem
merchant of Hiroshima:
Early in the month of the ripening plum
he answered the call of the rising sun
without sorrow.

To my mother convey this empty urn
enameled with gulls,
from Shimabara in the south.
Speak no word, bow twice, retire.

Do not look for the girl
with oval hands and eyes of jade.

There in amethyst
ahead of the first light,
the raven winged box freighted with fire.

May it be a mother eagle, proud,
pregnant with all her predacious young.

Sometimes when you burn
the ceremonial tapers and scatter

15

incense before your sons, remember,
my friend, how we locked fingers here
... last human touch.

Not yet nineteen I fly
only to dive into the sun.

SICK VETERAN

Swathed in the olive overcoat they issued
you at Kilmer the winter of '42,
toga-long and full—a touch of slapstick.
(They predicted you, a bare eighteen, some flesh
and stretch.) God but that cloth's endured!
tougher grained than nerves.

Your hands are gloved. Red hunter's cap,
bled pale, peaks low across your eyes
that cast whole world in shadow, won't
be caught. Noosing the upturned collar,
a muffler knots your throat.

Ninety degrees an August morning
your years again beyond the flash
that scorched to we give up those paper people
on the underside of earth and still you prowl
our streets, mummy whose bones won't quit
strutting though they're cold.

FULBRIGHT STUDENT

One Lounès Tagmount, ex-F.L.N.

with teeth of gold and
Charlie Chaplin smile,
whose finger ends in passing
look a little funny

because, his *compagnon*
Abdelaziz Saidji
will tell you over beer,
"un brigadier français ...
tous les ongles"
(here Aziz pantomimes)

who heard his sister's rape
"par les paratroupes," escaped
from *"les bourreaux"* by leaping
through a louvre, stole home
to find his mother dead—
"bombardement de représailles"

who enjoyed *"le plaisir exquis"*
of capturing *"le seul et même*
brigadier!" (here Aziz laughs
and fists the table) in a midnight
ambush near Laghouat and (now
Aziz' middle finger dances
in the air) surgically for

soul's sake, no anesthesia
for the nerves, yanked out
one *("unique")* fingernail

addresses me as *"Monsieur le professeur."*

THE BIRTH

I saw a pair of machines
come together one midnight
in a ring of blue-white light.
Oh! it was obscene

the way the long-nosed Buick
battering mounted the tail
of stopped Ford, with a shriek
of rubber, a groan of steel.*

A long gasp after the crash
had died, one last they thrashed,
grossly—as I imagine
rhinoceros in passion.

Blood rusty fluid leaked
to the street. How curious
after those carcasses
had settled, like two beached

whales a little apart,
to see something live come
crawling astonished from
the blackness of Ford's innards.

MAGNOLIA BLOOMS

For Gladys and Harold

You clipped lush sprigs from your blossoming
tree to lavish some fragrant spring
on us indoors. A fugitive

sweetness greeted us entering
our living room after an evening
walk. Heart-rooted offerings outlive

all blooms, like seeds. No little thing
in a time of self and steel to bring
flowers and graciously to give.

GEORGE WEIMAR WHO TAUGHT ME CHESS

Who knows how well the embalmer did
or how the chosen timber seasoned,
which route the rain runs rutting down
and which thawed snow leaks subtly through
precisely where they sank his shaft
and filled—some eighteen years ago?

No rain, no melted snow seeps in
the consecrated niche of mind
where icon-like by taper lit
he sits transfigured over play,
the black queen pendent poised between
the forfex of two fingertips—
some twenty-seven years ago.

ALBINO MORNING AT BARNEGAT LIGHT

Summer sun shows small as a winter moon
and paler and I see how sky is thin
white water, ocean is smoking space in
which our jetty wisps. Each ninth
lung heave fog horn howls "doom doom."

Smart weather for the laughing gull to work—
cousin of crow and vulture, brother of hawk
and falcon, shrill screamer after salt flesh,
needle-nosed destroyer in the shallows,
hooded executioner of surf fish,
sickle-winged assassin through the mist.

BEACHWALKING IN A STRANGE LIGHT

We footprint among vines
    of sea greens scribbling
foolscap sand with designs
    that might mean something—
like manic poets' lines.

Hove on bleached log a clump
    cryptic as a rune.
You scavenge tide's last dump
    for pear conch, blood stone,
while I store the whale hump

of my mind with color against
    a looming drift white
time on the Kansas plains:
    infrared west light
tracing purple on our veins;

cross winds from sea and bay
    splotching surf-half-mile
of ocean white-on-gray;
    a moth with green faille
wings felled by a chance-flung spray.

Lone heron gull retreats
    before our progress,
his giant outraged wing beats
    scoring this transgress
upon his sovereign beach.

I want to wander on
    seeing while you beachcomb;
but our cottage down the dune
    holds children not quite grown
still waiting for us. Come.

HEADLESS FISHERMAN ON LONG BEACH
ISLAND AT SUNSET

Sun spokes the inland sky.
A man stands in the shallows
fishing. From where I watch,
his slightly parabolic pole—
spun of first-line glass,
trimmed with rustproof hardware—
arches above the surf like any limb
a lissome Lenni-Lenape might slit
from birch or ash along the Delaware
in March and tote three days and nights
across the flats onto this sandbar
to lure and snag and fetch
the sly striped bass.

I doubt he casts so deep
as my springy savage—
his middle pregnant from prosperity,
back swayed, and arms and legs like logs.

The captain's cap (an Abercrombie?)
rides from my perspective smack
on his silhouetted shoulders.

MEDITATION

Nun on the Rocks at Cape May Point

He heaved these rocks I sit on, black
against their gray and saying morning beads,
upon the sands of this peninsula,
enclave of our continent, and bid
men pile and jetty them against
the ocean's swell, mossing their sea side green
to prove His constant labor.

Such stones might vault a vast cathedral
for Our Lady—St. Peter's rock—
and stronger stand against the storm
than poor St. Agnes by the Sea,
our little clapboard chapel duned
among mimosa wearing spray-like blows
and tall-stalked yucca whose bell-shaped panicles
bloom to carillons—our only campanile.

With lavish hand He salted all this water
and sowed it thick with fish—
eels that shoot electric; with fins
of green that gleam at night and jaws
that saw like breadknives; and some
in far-off seas, they say, that even fly.

The moon, He made it round-faced, bald
and dull of light. And still it tames

the sea for Him—what wonder! To show
His will He spills the waves on rock
and splinters them to spume.

One Sunday sunrise from this very jut
of stone I think I caught His face.
Ocean was furrow-less, smooth as a sky,
and there beneath its blue transparent skin—
a floating smile, not awful or forbidding
but as I picture whales, with jolly eyes,
huge brow, and little milk-white teeth.
I never told a single sister soul
and never saw, or thought I saw, again.
These nights I sleep with surf sigh in my ear.

Lord, render me useful for Your flow
as is the moon, ardent to break myself
upon Your rock; and let grace wash
as soft through me as foam. You capped
all black the heads of these white gulls;
so keep me hooded by Your marking will.

GULLS

When people go the hooded gulls come back
along these beaches where fall tides lick slick
all summer scars and architectures.
East wind erases too. Then winter works
some drama in the sand's shape: drifts, dunes, scoops,
hollows, shelves, breaks, and washouts. But always
smooth. For gulls leave only prints.
And in November gulls reclaim the shoreland.

At dawn their black and white decor
patterns a patch of beach into a chessboard
of bobbing squares. Swish!
a prestidigitator whisks
a checked cloth off a table . . . gulls
go flapping up the sky and shaking out.

With glasses I zero in one bird:
banking; pumping stiff wings to brake;
hanging motionless, head dipped,
as if on wires slung from a vaulted roof;
plummeting to sudden purpose hid within the sea
in which he spears. A beating of white wings,
gray water thrashed, a lifting spurt,
and there he climbs the air and skews
away . . . aimless, it seems.

That morning swaddled in mist the plane
on instruments over Boston Bay
projectiled in a thunderhead of birds,

29

sodality at wingtips. I own
those gulls' dumb terror, scarce felt
before birds whole sucked up the turbines
to annihilation, hones my imagining
as cruelly as the horror in the souls aboard—
ajump at thud of flock mass, catching
the engines' choke and wheeze on too much
gull life, lurching futile with the veer
and spin, gasping down the nosedown dive,
too macabre for any calculation,
to no bull's-eye in a riddled sea.

FRAZIL

Where cropped field folds cleft drain rain came
rushing to rock edge of land, ran
over, gushed all day. Sun done, run
thickened, stiffened, oozed so slow flow
scarce inched over verge till chill still
deeper struck. On scarp's stone lip drip
fixed, froze, closed sluice at last fast, past
running. Time can't race place; ice vise
holds, wins. So Earth's blood flood clots, stops.

ALL THESE ARE INSTANTS

All these are instants of no time—
long lost line
between my mother's breath and mine

at three the big hand hung on four,
five jumps more
till boy uncoiling springs the door

while new white stars spin high up sky,
red stars die,
through years of light we touch, love, lie

in chaos of images, void of word
still unheard,
joins architecture, closes chord

prairies of breath dwindle to line
cut off mine—
all these are instants of no time.

ATTIC DOLL

The patina of her face, flesh pink,
is pocked and peeled. One gouged-out eye
insinuates the wicked wink
of tribal god half blinded by

saint's thumb, then tumbled underground.
Like glacial fissure, from her chin
a curved cleft widens toward her crown,
where a boy might poke a finger in.

Hewn from a solid stock of cherry
her hands and fingers, feet and toes
never have bent. Too hard her belly
for impregnation. That girl whose

daughter she used to play became
for real a mother years ago,
then backed herself through birth again.
This child of wood, who could not grow

nor bear nor retreat through ravished past
to her beginning, survives crisscrossed
by time's stigmata . . . as idols last,
cocooned in ruins, while souls are lost.

JEOPARDY

Only under the high poised paw
can high heart hoist a falling sun.
Only during the fall of claw

and instant of gape of jag-toothed maw
can fell hand handle a crooked gun.
Only under the high poised paw

can poised eye measure the eye that saw
a lead bob plummet out of plumb.
Only during the fall of claw

can clawed ear hear a twitch of straw,
catch lightning lash of toad's whip tongue.
Only under the high poised paw,

the second of jut and snap of jaw
can taut nerve plucked, still tremble song.
Only during the fall of claw

can sleeper shocked from dream to raw
life live the heroic of a poem—
only under the high poised paw,
only during the fall of claw.

PRELUDE

The piano pupils of Miss Renn recite
in early June. While honeysuckle weighs
each breath within the concert room, sky grays
with swelling clouds. The girls are frocked in white.

One pledges faith to Beethoven—"Bagatelle";
one gives herself to Haydn—"Menuetto";
one plights a troth to Mozart—"Sonatina":
all vestal virgins of the virginal.

Each still a bud from which a fuller form
will flower; shaped like the neuter boy who bore
Zeus' cup. More innocent than Eve before
the Serpent crested, Leda before the Swan.

In turn proceeding to the instrument,
its bird-wing lid uplifted, they scarcely touch
the floor but seem to tiptoe air. A blush,
a fragile smile—the smile that wins child Heaven,

meaning no meaning other than a smile—
a breathless pause: then fingers run, trill, chord,
and turn the mighty harp. How vast the keyboard
ranges! When scored, how far from feet the pedal!

Finale's flourish, a resolving fifth,
a curtsy and diminished smile—each is done.
Waiting gallantly offstage, the tumid storm
now bursts. We nibble lady fingers, sip

a lemon ice. Shrill, a little gauche,
the chattering girls are startled by a clap
of closing thunder, like the stretch and flap
of giant wings, by a cleaving lightning flash.

PROPOSITION FOR SOUTHWARK

We'll hew it round, Will, round as the globe;
hang Hercules up on a wooden shingle,
World humped atop his back.

And flatter our good gentles into gods, Will,
viewing our vast suppose from seats near Heaven.
Apprentices for pennies in the pit—
we'll hoax these into heroes.

And hire men to sport themselves as princes
—ah, there's the jest of it, Will—
clowns anticking as shadows of ourselves
to laugh us through our English afternoons
till darkness rolls up-river.

And underneath the scaffold of this earth
witches will writhe; warlocks, goblins, half-men;
and apes and goats and toads; of course the serpent—
that hole we'll call Hell.

You be the swan that does the singing, Will,
and banks and soars within our wooden o.
The top—we'll keep it open to the sky
in case you need escape.

Then raise an ale house hard beside, where maids
a little wayward, sweet mead in cannikins,
the clinks of honest coin can counterchange
divinities to men.

From such brave enterprise we'll reap ourselves
a fortune greater than the Fortune, Will.

EMILY DICKINSON

A daughter among buttercups
whose father kept her fed
on dandelion drops
of wine and crumbs of bread.

Hers were absent lovers
garbed black as Bibles, all
too busy about her father's
vast enterprise to call.

Each lightning crack she sinned
after exquisite pain . . .
naked to the lashing wind
and ravished under rain.

She cadged from every sunrise
a kiss to seal election,
extorted from the butterflies
promised resurrection.

And set some crooked psalms
to syncopated airs
her neighbors eared as hymns
of praise and virgin prayers.

Now none of this would matter
more than shepherd's purses,
moss, or tadpoles but that her
strangled cries, soft curses

were caught between Mount Hol-
yoke and the Berkshires, where
we hear them echo still,
witching New England air.

CONRAD: A PASTICHE

While cresting wave and craving wind
he dodged the sun and watched the night—
no possibility of flight
from secret agents of the mind.

Sea spelled his Doom: to be the Mate
of splintered spars, of listing decks
the Master . . . through floating wrecks
and sunken reefs to navigate.

While able seamen daily drank
their measure of common grog, he quaffed
loneliness; each sunrise bitter-laughed
to see the seaways foolscap blank.

The silver of buried self he found
trapped in a jungle where brothers were shaped
of mud. This quicksand he escaped,
plundering much. Laden, half drowned

in a gulf of irony, he beached
on a live volcanic island with
an abandoned lighthouse, hieroglyph
of cigar-glow wisdom that he preached

in a tongue he scarcely spoke. Right hand
squeezed dark words from pen. Left gripped
a homemade detonator strapped
against his thigh like contraband.

READING YEATS ON THE BEACH

Sun renders his page a dazzling white,
Yeats' alphabet too blinding black
for eye to cipher naked against
sand glinting like some cyclopsian
mirror effulged by our closest star.

Smoked glasses help—as if the A's
and Z's were iron bars patterned
on the floor of a sun-filtered pool.

Then when beside me you, roused from
cat sleep by child's laugh, sit hostage
to silence, arms cincturing tucked knees,
and shoulder, sole shadow against sheer sky,
obscuring the poem, I fathom Yeats.

GUARD OF THE PISSARROS AND SEURATS

One afternoon in torment he jabbed
his sight nerve dead on points of yellows
reds and blues pricking by tens of thousands.

His realm now sound. However thief-like
your sole pads on his threshold he
rises from canvas stool, proffers
a face whose augered eyes screw in.

A certain axis vestiged in the arc
time and grave luck have sprung his spine to
argues some martyred sovereignty.
For future contemplation.

LINES FOR BRUCE MITCHELL,
LANDSCAPE PAINTER

Born Tayport, Scotland, 1908
Died Langhorne, Pennsylvania, 1963

To watch him reel across a tightrope,
high in a dream, blindfolded
by midnight, over a net-less pit,
without pole or parasol, was no fun.

Last night he slipped from
nightmare to dark peace and
now he knows what sleep is.
I for one refuse one tear
for this man raged for rest.

Best take him as sheer hand
married to knife or brush and
governed by a lens that prismed
chaos of a bungled universe
to lines defined, sharp shapes,
to tinges, tints, and tones more
just than light. The shivering
of that lens, the severing
of the hand that manned the tool
puts out our eye and amputates
our urgent power to do.

One landscape won't go away:
It's far in summer. Birds
show weary, favoring
bottom branches and the lower
sky. A river lolls behind
a line of willows. Perspective
is all harvest. Along
the nearer bank he chanced on,
almost secret among some
bramble, chicory, and burdock,
one stalk of late bloom thistle,
princely purple still though
touched with autumn umber.

Here scatter fragments of the shattered lens,
bury the hand still wedded to the brush.

BASS MAN

After a Drawing by Bruce Mitchell

The banjo player flails his five-string
like a flagellant in ecstasy.

Brass men ravish lip with metal:
one triple-tongues Hallelujahs
that march saints into Glory;
the other slides and glides glissandos
and buckles his back in prayer.

Or take the man with the tattooing hands
and the stuttering foot:
eyes goggle wild as epileptics',
head jitterbugs like rooster legs
freed from a brain by ax.

Nothing of *you* moves except the fingers
synchronized to pulsings of a heart
that ticks moon's tides, tempos
the wobbly dance of earth
and calls the interlude of stars.
Your eyes unblinking fix the axle of
all flux and in your ear sprung water slaps
against the walls of deep-sea caves
where human time lies drowned
and rhythm wombs.

CONJUGATION

Rilke's Duino Elegies *and Beethoven's Late Quartets*

"*Es muss sein,*" he wept, "*muss sein.*"
Unearthly music in a deaf ear.
Rilke too caught those echoes
spectral as tongues of the stars.

What terror, that recognition
high in an Adriatic castle!
And the heartwork: to wring
from the anguish of *Kindertoten*
somehow a joy; by will to annihilate
self for beloved's sake solely;
to harvest from speech seeds
of *Deutsch*—Necessity—an open
language of blossoms—Freedom.

And we in the din of lowlands
cringing behind dense lead and concrete
while betting on our bombs—dare we
dismiss such harking beyond limit,
where must and can and pain and joy
resolve, like twin nuclei
or galaxies firing into one?

FACE-SCAPE DURING SLOW MOVEMENT

While Mozart washes against the margin of
your cheek, half light and obliqueness of eye angle
accentuate its curve . . . as reclining in
a certain posture nude upon a couch
before a dove-gray arras you paradigm
white dunes against dun ocean.

During Adagio face flesh evanesces
until its contour floats unmoored to matter:
Eve's breast arched above Eden's fern fronds;
a hip of Earth flaring against rare space;
first Curve arced through Chaos.

Commingling currents of an undertow,
these modulating tones, tinges of light,
chromatics sift line to abstract fineness,
transfiguring your face.

STONE SCRIBE FOREBEAR

Your great great grandfather, you told
me once, while we sipped Oolong tea
on Hudson Street, carved gravestone legends.
And your father, as must his father him
and father's father too, you guessed,
had taken you at six or seven
to see his handiwork in granite,
surviving how many pictures and poems—
the overpopulated graveyard
in Southampton, itself a stone-ribbed corpse.

As you described his tools, bequeathed
to eldest child—the umber chisel,
crude as a lance some forebear gripped
in Lancashire; the maul, short-hafted
like a truncheon, with cobblestone
for head—I stared in ecstasy
at your white fingers circling the looped
bone china of the teacup and at
your wrist, blue-veined, flexed fluently,
and cinctured by the fur trim on your sleeve.

THE SEESAW

We face each other's end of the level board.
    On signal heave one leg across,
    bob grabbing hold the bar
and straddling hop on simultaneous.

An instant's poise before the magnet in
    the middle of the world exerts
    its claim. My feet find earth,
my knees deep-bend, uncoil and thrust to send

me shooting toward the stars, while you reverse
    direction, riding down the plank
    that drops you with its counterforce
until you smack the ground, recoil and yank

the seat from underneath me so I dip
    from somewhere near the sun. Our vaults
    and bounces build potential up,
like winding, till sprung lever catapults

the lead and nickle nub of self to space.
    Gasping we feel our gist flung free
    from its moorings to identity
still metronomed by time in a fulcrumed place.

Flesh maintains motion arcing on a point . . .
    an auto-propelled machine that soars
    and falls . . . of purpose innocent
as atoms or planets swirling stars.

Twin suns careening heaven's steppes, we swing
    the cosmos' poles, return. Then torqued
    from orbit specific self is jerked
back into body—a ball on a stretched nerve string.

Self weight diminishes. Our pendulum
    re-poised, bereft of energy,
    we die at equilibrium.
On signal heave to earth and density.

LIVING ROOM IN STASIS

A green globe tones the living room.
On the coffee table this morning's *Times*
proclaims our old diurnal doom
in *Iliad*-dwarfing headlines.

In a copper ashtray shaped like a heart
lie butts, time's white measuring rope
chopped into bits and smoked—the mark
of your lips blood red. A heliotrope

potted beneath the sill lofts leaves
toward sun, though now gold drapes are drawn
against the night. The rag rug weaves
a vortex pattern of braided brown.

The rocking chair rides its double keel
full steady. The hi-fi, with its arm
at rest and on its inert wheel
a captive quartet, still is warm.

Hot ashes bed the fireplace.
In a big brass kettle beside the hearth
a load of logs, apple and birch,
stands patterned black and white by bark.

The seascape opening up one wall
is a prospect carved from space impaled
upon the tip of time; and all
the painted people have just exhaled.

We sit at discreet distance, held back
from touch by dread of the little death
of afterlove. The room would crack
should either of us risk one breath.

WINTER MISSIVE

Come back once
while roses rampage through
the gardens of this village
desolate when last we prowled
its streets as our necessity.

Come back once
while laurel, each scalloped blossom
as delicately veined as
the underside your wrist,
lushes this hill, long gravely brown.

Come back once
while linden lofts its fragrance,
outrageous aphrodisiac,
across this air we breathed
in antiseptic winter, time of the knife.

Necessity assassinates all blooms
as brown prevails against veined white
as we must serve as surgeons of ourselves.
Yet once before the sweet cheat's gone
come back.

SEA RITE

Simmering haze smutched the sunset and we
    exchanged
the eye-words of the damned. A burgundy flush
on your wafer cheek decreed that lines estranged
as parallels might buckle once and touch.

The circumstancing time forced us to learn
a private litany toned low as night.
Orion died; we knew then we would burn
in the self-same circle when earth hove in light.

A shadow in false dawn you marked tide's flood
on the jetty while high up the dune I lay
and smoked . . . till sun, raised from a font of blood,
crimsoned our sand tracery for the priests of day.

LITTORAL

Spindrift awakens. Sun blinds
with largess of light. Child's laugh,

scud in a gust, splits Sound
to voices, gull mews, surf moan,

silence. Light modulates.
Eye limns the child beneath

the dome of sea blue sky,
against the space blue steppe

of ocean from whose troughs
combers accrue and crest

and plunge as these successive
images climb the fathoms

of my mind, then swell and ebb.
You are the ultimate

projector, a nub of flesh
in which no love can seed—

pulsing me like the moon,
dead mistress of sea motion.

AUTO-HARP

You supine, nude beside a bed
    of canna. Your brown
flesh earthy warm as petal's red.
    Serpenting down
your throat coils of black hair. Your head
    pillowing on the ground.

Lids closed against a smoldering sun,
    all unaware
that burning Barbary eyes have come
    upon you there,
you lift one strand and start to strum
    strings of stretched hair.

Auto-melodic. From that quaint lyre
    your playing wrings
mute music. Though my plucked desire
    a torment sings
as keen as were your fingers fire,
    my nerves those strings.

VISITATION

Ethel Dreifus, Domestic
Born 1886, Somewhere in Austria
Died 1958, Harrisburg, Pennsylvania

I

To come on you who nursed me more than any nipple
zipped in a zone of manufactured air,
ingesting oozes from a needle's nostril
down a hose out of a canted bottle,
sucking water up a pipe of glass

is to find you floating your beginning
in the ocean of the mother you many a time recalled
     to me
who missed her by a continent, a war, a generation

is to behold you hosting on some stranger's food
and potion, as Yahweh ate the herdsman's cake
and drank his milk within a tent
upon the plains of Mamre.

Oh, how many wells dug dry?
    how many sheep clean bled?
    how many deserts crossed?
    how many seas and rivers?

57

Oh, how many veils rent and trampled?
  how many tabernacles desecrated?
  how many cities lost and taken, ruined and
     rebuilt?

Oh, how many patriarchs bearded, old women ashed in
     grief?
  how many first sons gelded, daughters ravished,
     ripe bellies spitted?

Oh, how many crosses graced head down?
  how many wheels turned, screws twisted, racks
     stretched?
  how many bloody cloaks, empty chairs at tables,
     blank-faced graves?
Oh, how many cellars, attics, warehouses, alleys, sewers,
     caves?
  how many dungeons, cells, stockades, chambers,
     ovens?
  how many bullets?
  how much gas?
between the goatskin tent of Abraham the father
and this pavilion (plastic)
of Ethel Dreifus, scion?

II

Here where the eventual membrane capsules her,
a parasite on vital tanks and tubes, valves and dials
 (a telephone for confidant,

TV that exorcises loneliness for a dollar),
in a rented cube in a row of cubes
within a honeycomb of concrete, brick, and steel
ten floors above the labyrinth geometry of a city
chartered in a country gold with wheat and ribbed with
        iron
beside an inland river—

is this the Land of Promise?
the New Jerusalem?
the Inner Sanctuary of the Temple?

Why? why here
for Chosen Ethel Dreifus
to mortify through feeble crises:
contriving a turn, surmounting a bedpan,
negotiating between gown and sheet?

This lotion soothes, relieves, refreshes, deodorizes.
Kleenex disposes of what ought be disposed of.
And the practical irony of baby powder.

My grandmother died at home,
in the room where she and I were born.
Hers was not a swan's death, not a flower's.
By design she sucked from each of us a portion of our
        being—
so many drops of blood, so many pulse beats, so much
        breath—
and scored on each our hearts the figure of her
        crowning pain and terror.
You, Ethel, go antiseptically, alone.

59

My nurse's nurse:
>   "I want a good report tomorrow, honey;
>   behave yourself now, get lots of rest"—
a teacher to a kindergarten charge,
no, an attendant to a ward
too stunted to take in language
yet able to mark a tone, cipher gestures
and believe them true however crafted
for the visiting parents who pay.

I think the bird without a species
poised on his wooden breast atop a wire
speared in the scoop of soil the geranium
thrives in on the window sill will sing you
a death song sweeter than hers, Ethel Dreifus.

III

We two together—
a boy and his nurse grown man and infant
who neither sleeps nor wakes
but heaves, snores, gasps in protest
against the needle inducing life.

Let me slide my hand between the bars, gentle Ethel,
hoisted to contain mere fetal reflexes.
My fingers, let them sneak beneath the tent
folding atmosphere about you
as space globes air around our earth.
Let me steal in mine the hand that touched

me most when I lay barred and sheeted,
and measured against itself new growth and strength
as I now feel and weigh each numbered ebb.

Who? from black pits in yellow skull,
a voiceless plea, a silent quest for recognition.

Say:

> I am the first son
> among the twelve you who nurtured many
> never got a one of, little mother,
> come as a pledge against the finish of your sire's
>> seed.

Say:

> I am the father
> lost before your mind could store his picture
> come like Messiah, child,
> to claim and comfort you before the dark.

Say:

> I am Abraham
> come to take you to his bosom,
> my daughter, my bride.

As the nuzzle of lips on nipple
first catalyzes memory of returning features,
so wires within your fingers crossing wires
behind your eyes galvanize perhaps their fizzling spark.

IV

Undulating far across the city
a siren laps my ear.

I track its urgent tide along an artery
venting in this concrete heart
that pumps new life out, swallows old.

The other woman, bedded without bars
and using my air, catches our hands' embrace.
Through your transparent envelope her eyes
and mine collide, like underwater swimmers.

Hearkening to the howl's diminish
ten floors down, she knows herself
to be the one to live.

V

Late afternoon. I walk
an esplanade along the Susquehanna.
River locked, air biting.

Far from salt a gull
hovers above the ice,
screams, then wheels
up the crimson cone pointed on the sun.

AN EPITAPH FOR MY GRANDFATHER

My grandfather was not a handsome man.
Daguerrotypes show him even when young
to be fish-lipped, fox-eared, weasel-eyed, and skunk-
nosed. His pocketbook was a clamped clam.

His belch brewed the perfume of a sour custard.
His hand formed my first idea of fossils.
Bristles tufted from his ears and nostrils.
Oh, he fancied himself a tough old buzzard.

His father, he confided once without a smile
or tear, graced a lock of the Panama
Canal—tumbling drunk into a ladle of raw
ore, he alloyed a consignment of steel.

He exhausted three wives and assorted other ladies.
The first, my grandmother, died at twenty-six
of a ruptured lung, or heart. The second he bitched
fifty years; undid a third in his eighties.

But he was a great bridge burner! an even
greater scrambler back across charred bridges.
Giants his promises; his deliveries midgets.
No stauncher Christian this side of Heaven.

To his daughter he preferred a spayed spaniel,
and slept in his changed-weekly underwear;
then died of scant life in his ninety-first year—
no other epitaph save IRVIN DANIEL.

FRATERNITY

Father's first son had his mother
snatched from him when he was seven.
He was told she went to Heaven.
Heaven failed to send another.

His mother's hands as she was taken
clamped upon his heart and bruised it;
almost his tender shoot uprooted—
like a stripling apple shaken

loose from deep soil nourishment but
not felled. Married twice he never
found his mother's living picture;
somehow sired five daughters—scant fruit

for our father's family tree. No
learning fed his brain. Profession
practiced none—last bitter concession
granted at forty his seven-year ego.

For his lost birthright *my* mother
proffered care but failed to make up.
Here in peccant rhyme a Jacob
love I tender my half-brother.·

MY FATHER'S LOVER

At fifty years to feel her horny fingers
    clutch him there and squeeze,
as if she fed his manhood through the wringer
    of Mother's washing machine.

She griped him days on end, hours of the night,
    where sire least can bear.
As youngest son to have to watch him fight
    unweaponed against her

nearly unmanned my manhood on the way.
    Now all's dull peace inside.
Even he can't tell the hour, call the day
    or month that something died

privately, permitting his ravished will
    to yield to this last lover.
Meet and urgent for me here to chronicle
    father's passing from my father.

SONS AND FATHERS

Lurching the liquored night toward bed.
Against a tree on which our Jesus, I
stormed by snow swirls smacked my head.
Sweat rubbed from brow of squinting eye
smutched a palm wet red.

Wrestling wild wind on a bridge. Eye spied
my father martyred in currents, face
liquid black. Muffled by time he cried:
"Son, son! water is your race,
river your home tide."

Then tongue turned stone, too stone to speak
that Father broke flesh, that Father shed blood;
then sodden nerve bent weak, too weak
to answer call my father's flood.
Flakes flowed tears down cheek.
Scuff numb home sleep sleep.

AMONG THE AVOCADO TREES

Half blind, my mother in a rented room,
and I among the avocado trees;
my father in a madhouse, preaching doom,
and I at table with his enemies.

My brother picking pockets—a petty cheat,
and I a parasite upon a basking quean;
my sister selling sex along the street,
and I procuring love where toucans preen.

Before I headed south I passed the church:
no-trespass signs and padlocks sealed the doors;
the crooked finial—a pigeon perch;
blinding stained-glass windows—nailed-on boards.

The adjoining manse had been converted by
the local American Legion to a post;
a cannon on the lawn advised the Sky
it would brook no nonsense from the Holy Ghost.

Averting Heaven by the family fall
from Grace, here under Capricorn at ease
I lie and listen to the toucans call
and dart among the avocado trees.

PRODIGAL SON

Church of childhood—how many bombs
of my plotted and subtle intention have wracked
your shape these years! Yet you stand intact
in mind: My father among palms,

crow-robed, charismatic with the Word,
battering me guilty till beaten I
sin with the son who chose pigsty.
Unseen all-seeing eye God lurks

in the intricacy of ceiling beams
whose straight lines somehow conform to dome.
Hell brimstones in the boiler room
where, dazzling with sweated blasphemes,

a man of shadows stokes and rakes
white fires, one "Deacon" Buell, born slave,
handsome with power despite an age
kid arithmetic cannot calculate—

dark genesis of later lure
all underworlds will hold for me,
as the resolved geometry
of overheads will prove too pure.

No wonder—the in-between called life,
stained by sun through glass Christ on cross,
is oak pew, serge suit, scant grape juice,
crumbs of stale bread—I had to dive.

THE SIXTH DAY

My protozoan grandfather
helplessly potential as a star
floated salt seas for five aeons.
Moon weaned him onto tide, sun wooed
a spurt of will into a pseudopod.

Ambivalently my father
the amphibian dangled between
languishing soft ocean past
and laboring to mount strange Earth,
tough-nippled wet nurse of much to come.

Hence here now I
being precisely human
confess I feel the lash of vestige tail
and sometimes find myself on Sundays
sucking, like child on orange,
dream cravings for warm salt,
wanting to be maneuvered by the moon.

SELF-PORTRAIT ON MOUNT POCONO

My back is to the fire—birch and sappy
apple. Through a wall all glass I scan
copsed heads of hemlock, spruce and fir
eye-level with our lodge. Beyond,
the valley dips from view to where
a confrere slope ascends snow-blank,
upon which tree lines scribble like
the calligraphy of a certain Breughel
landscape, desolate of hunters.

Dusk slithering in transmutes the pane
to mirror that sifts things distant out.
At halfway night reflected flames
dance lambent on the treetops, as if
a prodigy: Ascanius' head
licked by the blaze of Providence,
old Yahweh burning alive in bush.

Though I the witness, gathering in
the dark dimension of the glass,
depict slight piety, scant dynasty.
Projected rather, when the beam
you flick on from a corner lamp
crossing fire's flare locates a second
center of perspective in the mirror,
like Picasso's Jaime Sabartés:
  ear wrenched toward eye
  eye tenterhooked on nose
  nose splayed on cheek
  cheek gashed by razored lips.

70

Such fractured physiognomy
illumines beyond x-ray, incises
past the scalpel, as if the mountain beds
had shifted opening fissures to
the gizzard of the world. And oh
what creatures writhe in those crevasses!

It's mercy in your hand to draw
the drape, curtaining off the climax of
some chthonic play. Then from behind,
your fingers touch to flesh again
and shape, my broken face.

AUTO-DA-FÉ

Call it our vesper rite.
I crumple the morning's *Times,*
lay twigs on, sticks, three logs
intersticed to deliver
the urgent tongues of fire.
You mix parts, four, of gin
(Gilbey's), of dry vermouth,
one (Pio), add ice, stir.
While I leak heat from match
to two unfurling corners
of the *Times,* you pour. No olives.

Mickey Mantle's cartilage.
Am Tel Tel ups, downs, net.
Sophia Loren's lips,
bald armpits, gartered thighs.
Yesterday's progress in
redeeming humanity
by napalming donkeys and kids.
The times-in-hope twining
of a long-stemmed flower from
Vassar College around
the keenest-honed saber in
the United States Military
Academy. Words on
words on words on words.

Wind heaved that limb's own heft
to cleave it from the trunk
of wild black cherry last

November. You stripped all
just hands could snap and I
ax-slashed the tougher stuff.
Four Sunday mornings we
obeyed the Lord a while
by making a bucksaw sing
His ways through tree flesh,
duped Adam's curse on our brows.
The relict copes with winter,
an amputated Y
among symmetrical
sycamores and maples.

Evening after evening
paired Grand Inquisitors
we commit the public past,
a certain stock of life
intimately our own,
severed, self-mutilated,
to fire. Unsheathed by flame
images flare clear: Dido,
pierced, jetting seething blood.
Clean-harnessed Beowulf
and alabaster Hector.
Three whole-fleshed Israelites
communing with a fourth,
sheer form—Jehovah as kindling
a bush. Young Christians dressed
in shirts of wax and fixed
to axletrees—slow bright
torches illuminating
the gardens of Nero. Naked
on live coals intermingled

73

with glass, St. Agatha.
Three Piedmontese—one Michael
Gonet, ninety, and Mary
Revello and Margaret
Pravillerin, ancient
widows, roasting by degrees.
The oven of Hiroshima.

We sip; tongues flicker, speak:
"Imagine yourself a brick
with full quick nerves. Imagine
the kiln stoked glowing white.
Imagine your flesh living
fire both within and without.
Imagine your melting eyes
goggled on running sand.
Suppose now your life continued
while you flame—from the instant
to moments to hours to weeks,
years, decades, centuries,
millennia, forever."
Sand dropping grain by grain.

Silent we sit and see
and hearken to the blaze
that does not burn for comfort,
and drink to quench within.